Going Home

Going Home

by

Nancy Richardson

Cover design by Shay Culligan
Cover photograph by John Anderson
Author photograph by Judy Brook

ISBN: 978-1-952326-22-6

Kelsay Books
502 South 1040 East, A-119
American Fork, Utah, 84003

You know the mind, how it comes on the scene again and makes tiny histories of things. And the imagination—how it wants everything back one more time.

—Richard Hugo

Acknowledgments

My thanks to the publications in which the following poems appeared:

An Everyday Thing: Finishing Line Press, 2018
 "Randomness," "Kent State Trial," "Myopia," "Shale Play,"
 "Pay Dirt," "Patience," "Bounced," "An Everyday Thing," "My
 Mother's Hunger," "Transaction," "Clarence and Anita,"
 "Fathers," "Door to Door," "Portland 1991," "Returning to
 Kent State," "Say," "Myopia," "Portland 1990," "Floater,"
 "Locusts," "Lost," "In the Cardiologist's Office"

Calyx: "Myopia"

Mobius: "Kent State Trial"

Plainsongs: "Transaction"

Teaching the Art of Poetry: "An Everyday Thing"

Dogwood: "In the Cardiologist's Office"

The Breath of Parted Lips II: "Youngstown, Ohio 1952"

Contents

If I Can Help You I Will

The Ghastly Water of the Swamp

Four Dead

They Bent the Words Back

Don't Get Hysterical

I Want to Go Home

Introduction

The poems in this book represent an American life lived in the latter half of the 20th century and the early years of the 21st. The poet brushes against the country's myths of equality and opportunity. From the smoked filled air of Youngstown, Ohio, to the halls of governmental power in Washington D.C., the poems document a personal, political, and historical record of a life spent in pursuit of justice not always attained.

If I Can Help You I Will

Work

At sixteen my sister worked in a department store,
twelve-hour shifts selling sweaters to Christmas shoppers.
Work is telling stories of how hard it was, and how you
made it out. *Most of us have jobs that are too small*
for our spirits, says Studs Terkel, and so work can be more than
a Monday through Friday sort of dying. I never thanked my
sister for working so hard. For always being poor and always
searching for inspiration. For stoking the fires, feeding the dogs,
teaching, and pacing. Or thanked my mother,
valedictorian of her high school class who worked
in a department store for $1.50 a day during the Depression
when she could not go to college with her friends.
For myself, who drew blood and cooked serum and walked
into sick rooms until I found another sort of life.
For Levine, who said work *is about waiting,*
shifting from one foot to another. For Akhmatova,
who suffered destitution but found life in poetry, and said,
this you call work... To catch ere it's flown...
Life is sly, but I take something from it. Yes, that is
what work is. Work is taking something from it.

Piercing

I draw close to the bedside
of the dying woman.

    Take the pipette and sip the serum
    so as not to get it in my mouth

Say, "this will not hurt."
Pierce her thin skin.

    in a shock of ill taste and acid.
    Put the test tubes in the water

Hope for the vein,
rope covered in thin paper.

    and inject the reagent into each one.
    Watch as the colors change.

This time a rose of blood.
A wince and penetration.

    Forget the ones with the vacant stares
    and the yellow skin.

Forget the red cells and the white cells
and the blood that is stuck in veins.

    And the blood that pours into the tube.
      And the woman, who laments.

Mail Girl

Along the three-mile factory line,
the men's whistles and cackles,
the oscine noise of crows.
I, skinny teenager, stumbled
through my first real job
in high heels and cramped legs
in the General Fireproofing plant
of Youngstown, Ohio. Cathedral
of making things. Concentrating
on the route, the claustrophobic
concrete walkway, work stations,
and the men staring. A sucking of the air,
the suffocation of a hissing threat.
Mail was so important then.
The reaching into and the taking out of.
The opening and the sealing.
Around every hissing corner I learned
they wanted the mail and something else.

Wings

Three young lepidopterists

He didn't come with us to catch them.
We were to bring them back,
gently lift them with soft fingers
from the sack of the net and lower
their folded bodies into the killing jar,
so as not to damage their wings,
which were holding more air than skin.
Small particles caught on our fingers,
dusted our eyelids with yellow and blue
translucent powder, as they fluttered,
danced in the naphthalene bower.
Their stiff bodies locked up their wings
as though they were saving something.
He explained how we should move quickly,
pin them to the board, so out-stretched
they would give the illusion of flight
under the glass of the frames he put them in.
Who knows what he heard in their wings.
Dozens of small engines, fluttering
of swallowtails, the skittering of wires
being pried apart and beyond?

I Am the Young Man

I am the young man, full of strength and hope,
Tangled in the ancient endless chain
Of profit, power, gain, of grab the land!..
Of work the men! Of take the pay!
Of owning everything for one's own greed.
    —Langston Hughes

Arlette is full of gratitude for having left
the hanging South, for the scarfer's job.
He tells his story of nights in the 40's.
He would nurse his leg burns, blackened shoes,
read by kerosene lamp, "my soul has grown
deep like the rivers." Cooling down
from the day's work under the open hearth
where the ladle touching the mold
was "just like the 4th of July, except we were right there."
Pig iron to steel to bridges, buildings, cars.
But the steel mills were sold to the highest bidder.
Into the pot went the copper pipes,
the two-story ladles, the scrap steel, perhaps
the lunker catfish in the dredged-out channel
beside the plant. Arlette is not bitter. He reaches
into his pocket, between his labored breaths,
hands me his card: *Arlette Gatewood,*
If I can help you I will.

Youngstown, Ohio 1952

I climbed the hill on my green Schwinn
at dusk when the air lifted enough
for me to see the fevered orange flush
of the open hearth on the horizon.
Tomorrow, it would rain ashes on
our '52 Chevy. Later on a field trip
to the mill, I walked on a catwalk
above the open mouth. The runoff
hardened into steel squares-the sour
taste of ash played on my tongue.
The men in hard hats were so close
their sweat turned to powder on their faces.
The cast heat rose and billowed my skirt
out in a small suspended parachute.
Later I lay on a blanket in the backyard,
floated in the haze that wanting makes,
lifted off beyond the yard,
beyond the gray sun imagining
a clear trajectory, a blue sky.

Pay Dirt

On my street of oaks and elms,
duplexes are gone to boarded
and secret insides, to copper strippers,
mantel busters. Streets now canyons
where rivers run in a thin brown milk.
My house with its yellow pillars,
a sunroom where my grandmother
tended her African violets. Small petals
blooming in every season, even in this city
in Ohio where the sky was a leaden haze,
where the soot was called "pay dirt."

Shale Play

In the Hampton Inn beside the skeleton
of the steel mills, men in T-shirts drink
their coffee before injecting chemicals
ten thousand feet below the ground,
fracturing the gray shale. In the lobby
dining space yogurt cups sweat in ice
and scrambled eggs quiver in the metal pan.
The parking lot is full. A billionaire is planning
to develop Mars-terra firma landscapes,
pink hotels, associated industries and iron-oxide
sunsets. Red planet evacuation site. Here
in the Ohio motel where the breakfast mess
is being cleaned up, the men have left
to pump black ooze. Trickling in after five,
they'll wash the guar, benzene, dioxane
from their boots. Drink to the Utica Shale.

Transaction

Tired of all who come with words, words but no language, I went to the snow-covered island.

—Tomas Transtromer

My Unitarian Minister was a counselor
in a transactional analysis where people
give and take, talk and listen in predetermined
scripts *I'm only trying to help,* or *I'm OK
you're OK,* each human interaction reduced
to its smallest and most mean-spirited essence.
So when I had dinner at his house, I was
not surprised that he frowned at his small
and stately wife for the coffee being cold
or that he was rumored to be having an affair
with a blonde parishioner as in *I deserve it.*
He consoled me once on my rose chintz couch,
touched my hand meaningfully, handed me
a card he had inscribed, the blue calligraphy
some prophet's words, *what greater thing is there
for two human souls than to feel that they
are joined together,* the words were linked like
small blue train cars, silent, unmoving on their tracks.
That's the trouble with scripts, words chained
to one another. When I heard the sirens one
Saturday morning it was them being carried
away, one dead the other lingering. When she
opened the door to his office and pointed the gun
was she tired of the words that had no language?
So there was the metal's click, the detonation,
his startled face, her hand turning to point
the gun at herself and the snow churning as though
a wild struggle had occurred and left behind
like fans the imprint of wings and feathers,
drops of blood and then a lifting off as though
love had been set loose.

The Ghastly Water of the Swamp
—Neruda

Street Money

Kerry Campaign Volunteers, Ohio, 2004

We are here to save democracy,
where the sky rains soot,

where street money flows.
The heroin addict with shaking hands

makes his calls and splits with his ten dollars.
The ceiling leaks toilet water.

We say, "some doors are too dangerous
to knock on, even in daylight.
Take off your jewelry."

Bounced

Kerry Campaign, 2004

We couldn't canvas without lit.
And then we ran out of chum, you know,
buttons and bumper stickers. Then
the rolling bosses thing happened.
The power washer from Iowa was replaced
by the coke addict from D.C. with the black
fingernails and the bad temper. The last time
I saw her; she was standing by a dumpster
smoking a cigarette. The Voter Protection
people came and put on a "training."
They divided us into smaller and smaller groups.
To groups of one. Busloads of travelers arrived,
wanting Starbucks and chicken Caesar salads.
A woman from Oregon called to say she
would pay for meals with her credit card.
We ordered the food and ate it. The card bounced.
That's what you can say about it.
The whole thing bounced.

Patience

The voting machines of Ohio

The poor breathe the quiet air of corruption
in the gymnasium where the voting machines sit,
stout, winking hulks. The screens dissolve in a storm
of snow. Votes float into errant flying digits.
Patience festers at the edge of the freeway.
Resignation waits in long lines.
The power brokers, riding cheap tricks,
say cheating in the service of liberty is no vice.

Door to Door

Let these people
not be home

let the flyers
blow away quietly

stick to the
chain link fences

let me not walk up
these concrete steps,
one more time

stand on this torn
green outdoor rug

read the Persuasion Script
promise life

will get better
perhaps not now

perhaps in some
other person's lifetime

Arson/Youngstown Ohio/1983

following Hugo's instructions on how to write a poem

*Make your first sentence interesting and
immediate.*

In the dark night the fireman perched on his
ladder truck, waiting.

*Never start successive sentences with the same
subject.*

When people die we close their mouths and
wait.

*The opposition is more dramatic if you don't
call attention to it.*

When houses die we let their bones stand in the
rain.

If you ask a question don't answer it.

Why did people burn their houses down?

*Often the dramatic can be at the end to good
effect.*

They loosened the stair treads and he fell
forward, fire everywhere and on his skin.

The Swamp

U.S. Department of Education, 1980

Down the hall the Assistant Secretary
holds a prayer meeting beneath a painting
of Jesus Christ. Clarence Thomas writes,
"turn civil rights over to Mississippi."
Reagan declares ketchup a vegetable.
I am bewildered here in the Executive Secretariat
routing memos for clearances and pondering
Neruda who wrote, *blow on blow in the ghastly
water of the swamp,* puzzling whether being in
or out of this muck will make a difference.
I had a naive friend who once camped
in the Everglades on a wooden raft in the mud
and at night she was attacked by swarms
of mosquitoes. The Assistant Secretary autopens
the Secretary's signature to a letter,
"this office is filled with secular humanists."

Clarence and Anita On the Way to the Seminar

When Clarence got into my car he slid
into the back seat waiting for Anita
to hurry it up. Anita chose the front.
On her face an expression
that every woman knows, a little fear,
a little anger, halfway wanting to please.
Being desired and disrespected
at the same time. A king in his carriage
in the car on the way to the seminar.
I drove and Anita sighed, the two of us
in service to his ambition as we weaved
through D.C. traffic, as he grunted
and crackled the New York Times.

Four Dead

Randomness

Kent State, 1970

She slid from her bed on the morning of May 4,
chose the bright red blouse for the occasion
of the day of her death. Sometimes I wonder
how my death will come, specifically the *like,*
the *what,* the *how.* Will it be after dinner when I rise
from the table, grab the hot wire of an infarct
across my chest, or after the tenth visit
to the cancer clinic where the vile brew delivered
through the pic-line turns my skin yellow, then blue,
then white. But getting back to her as she slammed
the screen door smelled the newly cut grass,
walked looking up at the pillowed clouds
and the man pointing the gun four hundred feet away
saw something extraordinary through his sight.
A dazzling red and gold flash moving in the parking lot.
A small sun come to the tarred surface.
I rise from my bed and offer to the gods of randomness
maybe, perhaps, if: life as hypothetical.

Returning to Kent State

In its countless alveoli, space contains compressed time.
That is what space is for. —Gaston Bachelard

In the grassy courtyard of the married student housing,
Derek and the Dominoes blasts in blue moonlight,
Layla you've got me on my knees. Just up the hill
voices from the Tri-Towers dorm float downwind,
can't stand it anymore. We feel the bullet holes
in the brick walls as we pass by. On the hill
the metal sculpture, another bullet hole, small tunnel
on the way to flesh. Pause and turn to see
the scattered bodies in still poses, in memory
lying in the grassy meadow. Daniel Berrigan
marching, just out of jail, his hair flecked gray.
The scent of candle wax, low voices murmuring.
Bill Schroeder's parents standing in his spot
in the shadow of a tree, candlelight casting
shadows on their strained pale faces.

The Ill Paralegal

She sat on the floor, rifled through the box
of evidence. Manila folders, fading photographs.
Something about a conspiracy. Something about
who set the fire. One gesture that might have made
the difference. She, student of what had been.
Recovering the bricks of disaster in redactions,
facts buried in the small squares of black ink
stacked line upon line in perpetual possibility.
One day at lunch a joke about the dead man
is out of my mouth too late to call it back, and her face
is like a child's just after the fall and before the tears.
I change the subject and she lets it go, focuses on
her corned beef sandwich. So much for what might
have been, what if, what will be. Here in this lunch place,
the past is irretrievable and the future is this sandwich,
the dripping pink beef, the mustard's rebuke.

An Everyday Thing

Notes of the students' lawyers, Kent State Trial

one round was fired on the hill.

what did they say?

you can see smoke in the pictures.

good hair, the jury likes him.

find the impeaching part.

cause she's so pretty.

watch out for hearsay and conclusions.

did you see anyone carry any bodies?

he put the blame on me for his fuck-up.

you have any phenobarbital?

he gave the order to kneel and take aim.

if he hadn't heard the order to fire.

he's getting scattered, tell him to sit down.

can you help me cash my paycheck?

one person in troop G emptied their whole clip.

he's been ineffective lately.

the net gain is clearly worth the cost.

he had his hand on his holster.

Bill was not dead there.

I yawn to mask my true sentiments.

when you play in the mud you get dirty.

say thanks to Charlie.

isn't death an everyday thing for everyone?

he said if they rush us shoot them.

Fear

Kent State gymnasium, 1970

The air is thick with strobe lights and sweat.
On stage Jefferson Airplane sings for the four dead

and the nine wounded. Gracie Slick in a voice
like a dirt road, *we are outlaws in the eyes*

of America, tear down the walls. Behind her on the screen
Jeffrey Miller's body leaking down the concrete in blue

staccato lights. Somewhere a door lets in a gust of fear.
Tear down the walls won't you try?

But trying's getting ready to run in fear's leather boots.
I screamed, punching the blue mist.

Kent State Trial, 1975

"The photos speak for themselves,"
said the Judge to the students' lawyers.
The jury puzzled over them, but the photos
lost their nerve. In this one the Governor
would shout, "worse than the brownshirts
and the communists, night riders and the
vigilantes." Or another, blue sky, clouds, a clot
of guardsmen huddled in the field, perhaps
a picnic on a spring day in May. If the photo had
bothered to listen it might have overheard
their plans to turn in unison and fire. But
it was busy and they were whispering.
Here now tongues should be wagging,
"the guardsmen turn and level their weapons,"
and the "guardsmen shoot. All together now,
Fire!" But the words were prisoners
in their cells, banging their tin cups against
the metal bars. The photos went on in silence,
in cardboard boxes in wet basements.
The photos held their tongues

They Bent the Words Back

Naming

This is the way you do it you say *look at me*
and hold the ball and then you say *ball*
and you point to the ball and if she gets it right
you say *good girl* because it is good
to learn language when you have none.
Some say we are born with language curled
in our brains unfolding. But she had not one neuron
that would help her. If she faltered we would do it again
and again and when the word ball was mastered
we would say *is this the same, show me same*
language ratcheted to concept. Each concept, word,
same/different, traced in the ink of repetition.
Imagine you are looking at a face and you can see
only part of it, perhaps the ear, and the ear is talking to you.
But you see the ear and then you see the glass lamp
on the table and that lamp is shiny and is talking
in words you cannot name and you cannot tell
if your own body is here or in the lamp. Mothers
are fraught with naming *this is a light, see the light.*
If language does not come we teach *say ball,*
point to same. You name, therefore, you are.

Water

Water of creeks in the park
drinks on the counter, insatiable

desire for wetness. Water
the soothing touch, lullaby,

cradle rocking. Hush small child
of misfortune. We will teach you

to make the sign for love, the sign for water.
We will give you love and water.

And when you leave on the bus
for the nursing home where you live

we will wave to you and you will
sign, *please water,* return to me
what is lost.

Teacher

I can hardly speak about it now.
The times I spent with him.
His small body and his face
pock-marked from his own quick punches.
He was a being within a being:
one in chains, linked to the other,
the whipping boss. I heard years later
that he kept trying to escape.
But his affliction lasted. I think back
on that time when I too was looking
for a quieter self. An inclination
that dissolved like tissue paper in water.
I know that I reached, met his calmer,
captive self, when we sat on the hill
overlooking the water, when quiet
made a room and he breathed in.

Bending

Maria Clark Condos

A resident said he heard
no laughter in the dust
no whisks of wind in the dark.

Just the quiet of tall ceilings.
And a remade thing.

Once a school for cast-off children,
their words twisted into the farthest
reaches of language. Here, they bent
the words back.

First Dance

Eric's eyes were on the ceiling
and the silver, blue, and red
floating balloons overhead
like the mystery stars
in the winter sky in Maine.
Some things look
like other things he thought,
as he swayed, head tilted.
Flashes and auras,
illuminations
from the far side of vision.

Say

The slant-light of winter
through tall windows
where music plays.

We make bird-houses,
read stories, eat fruit.

Their small eyes stare up
into my safe face, not a face
attached to smacking hands.

Hands that would make you want
to take your clothes off,
rub grease in your hair,
jump out the window.

I sit across from each child,
say *look at me—this is a red apple,*
say *apple* say *water this is water.*
Say, *I will remember you.*

Unbound

We thought of holding her
to the earth with a small rope,

gawky human kite bounding
around the schoolyard.

In the end she remained unbound,
running for that necessary moment

when the earth left her
with all of its weight.

Dare

Bruno Bettelheim is yelling at me across
the panel of experts in Bangor, Maine,
in 1976, and he has a thesis on autism.
Somehow, mothers have created blankets
of frozen emotions, wrapped their children
in them, and created a brain disease.
By the 1990s, he is exposed as an abuser
and a fraud. But for now, in response
to my challenge, he says, "How dare you,"
purple with rage. And I say, "I'll take your dare.
I'll tie it up, put it in a room and leave it
there, occasionally dropping by
for a little talk therapy, mother theories.
And when it misbehaves I'll pull its hair,
scream at it, turn purple."

Hold

Because the school bus stops,
lights flashing, in front of a
beat-up trailer, plastic toys,
odd junk sprinkled across
the snow. Because a young boy
exits the bus, walks to the door.
A friend says, why give him
your time? I say, it is a tricky thing,
hard to carry. You hold it tight
or it slides away.

Don't Get Hysterical

Myopia

Who could live with a person
who sells vacuum cleaners to
old ladies, sweeps the dead
skin from their mattresses,
promising them a cleaner life?
All I felt was the heat on his skin.
Later in the dark, when the baby's cries
were like spikes in the mattress
and he wouldn't get up, I wanted
to throw his body off the bed.
Words float away like dust motes
leaving nothing but quiet air,
the way the small silences around
a conversation alter the direction
of thought and are seen, like dams
in a river, by the way the talk flows
up, over and around. I sat in front
of the TV serving the babies chunky
food from jars the day Robert Kennedy
was shot, sobbed for his lifted head,
his empty eyes, my silent life, and left
then, along with the unused words,
drove down the two-lane road in my
rusty Volkswagen with the kids, headed
for *insight, foresight,* some other life.

My History of Guns

My skeet shooting husband pulls a pistol out of his stocking drawer...

John Kennedy is shot with a Mannlicher-Carcano rifle...

The luncheon at the Cleveland Athletic Club the day after Martin Luther King was shot and Robert Kennedy speaks in an emotional and shaky voice...

Robert Kennedy is shot with an Iver Johnson revolver in a hotel kitchen in Los Angeles...

The Vietnam War and nightly broadcasts of soldiers ripped apart by guns, napalm burned children, and the My Lai massacre...

The Kent State shootings of students with M Garand rifles and an M1911 pistol. Sixty-seven rounds in 13 seconds. Thirteen shot, four dead in Ohio. My brother-in-law shot for raising a finger, another student for wearing a red blouse…

My faculty advisor shoots himself in the head in 1974 and dies...

My Unitarian Minister is shot in the chest by his wife in 1975 and dies...

A friend's son tells me that here in America carrying a gun is a right. Conceals and carries. Those people in the city are going to come for him one day to his gated community with the fake lakes and clumsy houses. He will be ready.

White Wild Horses

The white, wild horses' mouths gaped.
Their hooves clawed the air

and I at two was lost
among the carved white legs

of the carousel my father put me on.
Left in a forest of knees and teeth.

I cried for being lost. This first memory,
signifier of all leavings.

Now I take the child I was in my arms,
and say to her "there will be others

who will ride with you,
on the wild horses."

Shades of Love

He was always looking for the right kind of
love. We went to Haiti one late 70's January on
a lark, where Papa Doc and the Tons Tons
Macoute had the kind of power that scares the
air. The hills around Port a Prince were sliding
into the rivers like brown milk, the trees cut
down for charcoal. On the street of legless
men, thin women, children lifting up their arms
to us, we slept in a pink hotel, red with sun and
fevers. We dined at LaRecif, Chez Gerard,
fictional restaurants with no running water,
glasses washed in basins by candlelight. Years
later I do the math. He is seventy-six, too old to
still be looking for love, perhaps not here at all,
floating in someone else's memory, but
yesterday we were driving through.
Four million people on the streets-four million
people looking for food, and I glance over at
him behind the wheel as he honks and winds
our way through the mess and I think,
there are shades of love. The kind that fills up
every excavated place, and then the kind that
drifts, like grey smoke, translucent, years away.

He Said

You cannot change me.

I'm going to fill this cavity without novocaine.

I'm not sure I love you.

How does it feel to have spent so much time and come up with so little?

You will have to use your husband's credit card.

You never stop talking.

What you need is a good...

Why are you still mourning? It has been a year already.

You can't do that.

You are the worst patient I have ever had.

Sew this button on.

Don't get hysterical.

Let's forget about that and do better the next time.

Calm down.

The Edge

for Galen

Just before sleep in the old mattress
with the sinking center, we whisper
teenage talk, not of our futures
but who the boy is who loves her
in real life. I dream of falling
but her legs catch me in a scaffold
of bone and flesh. In the dream
she bends low over the blueberry bushes,
and the warm June air forms a mist
in the room like fog. It is not anything
for the last time that pleases her,
but the ordinary things of each moment's
invention mean there is no history in which
to place the edge, she must slide over.

Mothers

For Thelma

She said, "Find your sweet place."
In her white starched dress,
she rode the bus through town,
stepped down to our three-bedroom duplex,
having left her own child daily
for four girls in need of mothering.
My mother put on her suit
and rode the bus to her sweetest place,
work. So we had two Mothers.
Each carrying us in baskets of necessity,
and the weary things that women say
to each other in that violet hour.

Fathers

Once when we were twelve,
playing cards in my living room,
she whispered, *my father
comes to me in the night.*
She said, *first the footsteps,
then his hands.* She learned
to float above herself, look down
on the bed. And I, my father
having left us, thought this must
be what fathers do. Leave your life
or push you from your body.
Daughters hovering, waiting
for the sheets to be quiet,
or at the window looking
down the street for his walk,
his pale hands reaching out for you.

Portland, June 1991

I am sitting on a makeshift terrace
in Oregon in June.

There are six of us.
Our talk is the conversation of waves,
more movement than meaning.

There is a garden in front of us and this;
the smell of mock-orange blossoms,
petals drifting over us, away
and falling on her skirt, my sister's skirt.

She looks up.
Her face is flushed and oily.

Our words fall into the air one by one.
Something important or not is being said.

She drifts, halfway into memory now.

She is turning into petals and warm air.

Beads

A friend of mine, long dead,
gave me a necklace of prayer beads
from Korea.

Sometimes I rub one
to remember him.

Years ago, I was married to a man for eight years.
The thing is, I can't remember him
except that he talked without knowing.

He died speaking tongues,
member of a Pentecostal church
in a shopping mall in Arizona.

His fifth wife sent me a package
of old jewelry, assorted necklaces
that she thought belonged to me.

I struggled to remember me in another life,
wearing cheap, fake-gold beads.
But those clunky beads,
belonged to someone's other life.

Lies

My political economy class
spent a week on lying.
White lies, half-lies and whole lies,
intermittent lying, necessary lying,
silence. According to research,
an entire country's government might
be brought down by one lie. More often
people's lives wind up on the scrap heap
of trust. My Presbyterian minister stressed
that *Thou Shall Not Lie* was a living thing
like an organism attached to the soul.
I did not lie. My mother did not lie.
My sisters and I were too busy talking to lie.
My father was a lie, personified.
But I learned the culture of lying later.
"I'll always love you" was a favorite.
"This won't hurt" another. But what is life
if not one big negotiation with the truth?
We learned that good faith in negotiation
is a necessary condition for bargaining.
So truth, are you honest?

I Want to Go Home

In the Obituary

Love is so short, forgetting is so long.
—Pablo Neruda

His face seems to have melted
Eyes to cheeks, cheeks to mouth.

He is smiling. Years ago
we loved.

He repaired motorcycles, played the guitar, lost
in a gentle, drifting cloud of uncertainty.

Dear Mr. Fantasy, play us a tune
Something to make us all happy.

In memory I imagined him on a farm
his blue eyes and his body working

fields of hay. Or racing his black Norton
on asphalt tracks. But the obituary tells

of a life on the water. A sailor.
On the Chesapeake and the Caribbean.

Did he ever hear my voice in the wind?

Steel to Dirt

If there were a Museum of the Fifties,
it would feature art of steel,
tinny finned cars, slab-sided buildings,
and wax-figured men in hard hats
who stood so close to fire their faces melted.
Some nights I sweated the uphill climb
to see the open hearth's glow
on the horizon, as if the fire were holy.
On summer mornings the train whistle sighed
and the sulfur air cast yellow shadows that
I washed away in the public swimming pool.
where the diving boards hung, flapping
over pewter water. There is a way
of growing up that comes from breathing
ash and the weight of steel holding you
in place. Now the gray mills coil
like sick snakes along the river. Everything
burns eventually or melts, steel into dirt.

Listing

All time is unredeemable
—T. S. Eliot

The old woman walks up the dirt road
in front of the brown house with the wide porch.
The observer on the porch sees her pass in front
of the barn's silvered door, the rusted truck
resting against the old garage. Charley's dead
brother's truck. The observer on the porch thinks
time will take the old woman as it has the rusted
truck as it has Charley's brother. The old lady,
white hair pinned back, red sweater swaying.
And Charley's brother's truck listing. The porch
is now gone in a house fire and the observer
has faded into old age. The old woman died after
her daughter shuffled her among cheap nursing homes.
Charley is sailing. The old garage was torn down
by the hedge fund owner who torched the house.
He raised the old barn twenty feet and stored
his antique cars there. The observer thinks
that time is finished when a 200-year old house,
the cradle of years, can be razed by a billionaire hiding
his assets beneath the barn floor in the poorest town
in Vermont. The barn teeters on its high heels,
a warning to old barns everywhere.

In the Photographs

She is holding one of the children.
He is holding the dog. She is smiling.
His face is a question mark. Some people
need to see the midnight clock, not think
the hands are out to get them.

He ascended the goodbye ramp,
made a life of cheap hotels in Jamestown,
Erie, Buffalo, sold desks to secretaries,
measuring their legs for the perfect fit.
In 1980 he lay alone on the floor for three days
before they found him.

Some people live inside others,
their faces look out in recognition,
their shadows move.

He lived inside himself, pulled his shadow in.
The wedding photographs, the blossom bouquet,
the four children and the Tudor house.
The tilt of the head and the smile
that never fit the corners of his mouth.

Metta

Lovingkindness

Metta to oneself: *Was it really me, then, how can I say I'm sorry.*

Metta to the Benefactor: *He said, you are the way you are.*

Metta to the Dear Friend or Family member: *Dear friend of long ago, don't fall again.*

Metta to the Neutral Person: *I hear you cleaning the bathroom, your sighs, the strokes the sponge makes on the tile.*

Metta to the difficult person: *Thinking makes it so.*

Directing Metta to all beings: *Breathe in.*

My Mother's Hunger

After dark she would sneak into the neighbor's garden

  pulling the string on the overhead closet light

stomach aching, feet swollen

  there were shoes of every color and material

Looking up at the stars, she would wonder
how she had become

  dark leather pumps, some

so small. The world with each sunrise

  in shades of pink and yellow, silk or linen

was a dread she tasted like salt. She felt for the

  boxed and shelved nylon stockings in plastic

sweet tomatoes, her fingers searching down

  bags, shades of taupe and cream or gray

the vine, the round and fleshy globes, lifting each one

  sequined dresses in black and crusty blue and

juice mixing with her tears spilling

  billowy silk in the closet's warm air

In the Cardiologist's Office

A *Whiter Shade of Pale* comes on a sort of 70's musak
version and memory that unwelcome guest visiting
and staying around too long wants to keep talking
and I am waiting for an echocardiogram a sonar picture
of my heart the thickness of the walls the synchrony
of valves the slushing of the beats and I am back there
the night before the accident by a lake and I see the moon hear
the soft slap of water and the song *her face at first just ghostly
turned a whiter shade of pale* and in the dark see his
white teeth his long brown hair and feel how uneasily he
rides risk's edge and the next day the car hits us on the Norton
and he dies in the road and what I can say about it is I keep his
orange plaid shirt for thirty-nine years and his prayer beads
from Korea and the song when I hear it and at first it is
the pain the clenched neck muscles where I fell against him then
the dizziness *the room was humming harder as the
ceiling flew away* and then just the dark weight of him my
hands circling his chest spinning *cartwheels cross the floor*
my head against his back bracing at the place where the car
crushed his heart.

Floater

Somewhere between a shimmy and a glide
the motorcycle wheels reach for road,
as her arms reach out and clutch his
jacket's black leather skin, as the
sun's heat sits below the stirrups, melts
the blacktop tar. The motorcycle glides
like a boat in a swamp and the sun
is also in the eye of the car's
driver from the east, who stops to turn
into a street so ordinary that its
concrete lawns are edged with chain-link fences,
and in his eye there is a floater,
a small speck in the vitreous of the road
and sky. The motorcycle driver who is
high on marijuana and therefore slow
to respond to the shifting signs
of the car's indecision, decelerates
and shouts something to her, but the wind
scatters the words and she is thinking she
forgot not to let someone else lift her up.
Hoist her feet off the ground.
When she was six her sister put her on
a rope swing that was so high
she hung there swinging lamely, losing
traction with each twisted arc, and so
remembers the risk in letting the wind
scatter parts of you through the trees
like the sun's diamonds.

Locusts

One hot July night when I was ten,

when my grandfather walked me around the
park,

when hot misty air hung in the shadows under
the street lights,

we came upon a tree blanketed in seventeen-
year locusts,
great brown piles of them,
some crawling out of their shells,
moving over others in a slow death dance.

What did I know of death?

That it might look like this,
crawling creatures, empty shells,
waiting to be stepped on,
ground into fine brown powder,
blown away with the wind?

What did he see that night?

His heart failing, breath raspy,

Perhaps not death, but the way things fall
away, transform;
shell to dust, skin to air, breath to stars.

Floating

away from the dock
the children's voices
calling

into the deep channel
rubber raft
drifting

away
white limbs on dark water

Mother
on her death bed
calling
"I want to go home"

eyes seeing white
behind the lids

in that still place
in the water

voices calling
come back, come back.

Enigma

Mother is dying in a small house in Ohio and in a dream
she has traveled to a large party of friends and relations,
living and dead. Her clothes are with her, shoes of cream,
dresses of sequins and chiffon, and a large bag of nylon
stockings, since they had been rationed in the war and who
can tell? In the dream she is stuffing the clothes into garbage
bags. Her daughter, 10 years dead, is helping her and as the
pushing of the clothes goes on, she tires and falls asleep on the
dream bed. She sits up and says, "I want to go home," but she is
in her real bed and in her own home and Elgar is playing
in the background. Her second daughter is sitting in the room,
writing a poem for her, which has the music as its hidden
theme:

Enigma Variations

"She strained to find the hidden theme,
enigmatic ribbons winding over
and around inventions simple
as a nursery rhyme. She, too had outrun
reflection, worshipped at the alter
of false starts. Allegro, presto andante,
eyes closed, she listened as the music moved
through its own life."

Her daughter ponders the thought that all lives have secret,
brambled paths and that Mother's path was her own invention.
Her daughter says, "you are on your way home now," and
touches her with the music.

Mending Time

How many days
must she have sat here

drenched in champagne light,
her heart a well?

I see her now lying
in this meadow

her fingers stroking
grass, mending time.

We think we exist
in other's lives

even in absence,
but the truth is

we breathe the warm air
of forgetting.

Lost

I am lost in the woods following a dead-end trail,
my ability to bushwhack up the steep hill in front of me
in doubt. Sit down, ponder the lost path. I sit in a patch
of moss and think. This wandering. Getting old.
Mr. Kinney lived to be 90. Did his work. Then said,
"I'm all used up," and died. And what about the sky?
Look up. Voyager, starship wandering in space
for 35 years doing its own work. Photographing
the rings of Saturn, the volcanoes of Venus, the moons,
Io, Delphi. Voyager has just entered the heliosphere,
a space where there is no reach of sun, no solar wind,
only remnants of stars millions of year old. Into the quiet
zone of no wind. Work done, battery depleted, no return.
This is where all journeys will end, in a place of windless
spirit particles. The sun hits the spruces, red pines. Breath
coming back, body heat down from cool moss. I get up.
Retrace the steps on the trails marked Slough,
Circumferential Dell. Find the intersection where I
went wrong. Where I chose the dead-end path. There it is.
Hidden in green. Fern Walk, the path I came in on.

Notes

"Love is so short, forgetting is so long*"* in *The Obituary* by Pablo Neruda from *Tonight I Can Write.* Quotations in *Work* are from the following: Studs Terkel in Goodreads quotes; Philip Levine quote is from his poem *What Work Is;* the Akhmatova quote "so this you call work," from her *Collected Works* and from lyrics to *The Trackless Wood* by Iris Dement; Richard Hugo's instructions in *Arson* from *The Triggering Town;* Pablo Neruda quote in *The Swamp* from his poem, *The Dictators;* Langston Hughes quote in *I Am the Young Man* from *Let America be America Again* and "my soul has grown deep like the rivers," from *The Negro Speaks of Rivers;* Bruno Bettelheim poem *Dare* refers to his book *An Empty Fortress;* "That is what space is for," from *Returning to Kent State,* is from page 18 of Gaston Bachelard's, *The Poetics of Space;* notes in *An Everyday Thing* are actual notes of the lawyers at the Kent State civil trial; the poem *Randomness* refers to the shooting of Sandra Scheuer who was shot wearing a red blouse on May 4, 1970, at Kent State; *Fear's* epigraph concerns the setting of the concert in October of 1970 after the shootings and song lyrics are from Jefferson Airplane, *We Can All Be Together* by Paul Kantner. Statements in *Kent State Trial* are trial and newspaper transcripts from *The Kent State Coverup* by Kelner and Munves; the epigraph in *Listing* is from Eliot's *Four Quartets.*

Lyrics. "Tear down the walls" from *We Can All Be Together* by Paul Kantner of Jefferson Airplane in *Fear;* lyrics from *Layla* in *Returning to Kent State* are by Eric Clapton. Lyrics in *The Obituary* from the song *Dear Mr. Fantasy* by Steve Winwood and Eric Clapton. Lyrics in the *Cardiologist's Office* from *A Whiter Shade of Pale* by Procol Harem.

About the Author

Nancy Richardson's poems concern coming of age in the rust-belt of Ohio during a period of decay of the physical and political structures that made the region once solid and predictable. The poems chart the shifting of the foundations upon which a life is built and the unpredictability of events that have profound personal and political consequences. Her poems in this book venture from the Ohio foundation to record a life of teaching and working for justice in many jobs and forums.

Nancy's poems have appeared in journals and anthologies, and her first chapbook, *Unwelcomed Guest* was published in 2013. Her second chapbook, *The Fire's Edge,* focuses on the events that occurred in the rust-belt of Ohio from the late 1970s onward. Her poetry book, *An Everyday Thing,* expands the narrative of that time and place and focuses on the effects of the period's dislocation years afterward. That book received a Kirkus Star and was named one of the Best 100 Indie Books of 2018 in all genres.

The poems in *Going Home* have been selected from these previous volumes and combined with new poems in a memoir that brushes against the poet's life working for justice in education and government.

Nancy lives and works in Vermont. She has an MFA in Writing from Vermont College of Fine Arts, an M.P.A. in Public Administration from Harvard University, and a Ph.D. in Education from Kent State University.

www.ingramcontent.com/pod-product-compliance
Lightning Source LLC
Chambersburg PA
CBHW070335090426
42733CB00012B/2482